IRISH FAMILY NAMES

WALSH
BREATHNACH

IRISH FAMILY NAMES

WALSH
BREATHNACH

Dáithí Ó hÓgáin

GILL & MACMILLAN

Published In Ireland by
Gill & Macmillan Ltd
Hume Avenue, Park West
Dublin 12
with associated companies throughout the world
www.gillmacmillan.ie
Text © Salamander Books 2003
0 7171 3553 5

Published by arrangement with Salamander Books Ltd, London

A member of **Chrysalis** Books plc

A CIP catalogue record is available for this book from the British Library.

9 8 7 6 5 4 3 2 1

All correspondence concerning the content of this volume should be addressed to
Salamander Books Ltd.

THE AUTHOR
Dáithí Ó hÓgáin, MA, PhD, is Associate Professor at University College Dublin,
Ireland, where he lectures on Irish folklore. He is the author of over 20 books,
several of them in Irish, on aspects of folk culture, history and tradition. He is also
a noted poet and short-story writer, and is a well-known conference lecturer. He
has participated in the production of documentary films in Europe and the United
States, and is a frequent TV and radio broadcaster.

CREDITS
Project Manager: Stella Caldwell
Design: Q2A Solutions
Picture Research: Julie McMahon
Cover Design: Cara Hamilton
Colour reproduction: Anorax, UK
Printed and bound in Italy

Special thanks to Antony Shaw for his invaluable advice and generous assistance in
writing the section on modern members of the family.

CONTENTS

INTRODUCTION

THE HISTORY OF IRELAND IS
A GREAT DRAMA OF WAR,
INVASION, PLANTATION,
IMMIGRATION, EMIGRATION,
CONFLICT AND SOLIDARITY.

INTRODUCTION

Above: The entrance to the passage grave at Newgrange in County Meath is a fine example of Neolithic architecture.

People have been in Ireland for about 9,000 years but, for over two-thirds of that time, what they called themselves either as individuals or as groups is unknown. The Celticisation of Ireland had begun by the fifth century BC, and a few centuries later it was complete. This process must have involved the coming of some influential groups from Britain and perhaps from the Continental land-mass. The Irish language developed from the Celtic spoken by these, and all our earliest surviving system of naming—whether of people or of places—are in that language.

From references to the country in ancient Greek and Latin sources, and from the earliest written traditions of the Irish themselves, the names of important early population groups in the country can be postulated. Since the country was known to outsiders as Éveriu ('the land'), the fusion of indigenous peoples and early Celtic settlers was termed 'the land-dwellers' i.e. Éverini or 'Iverni'. Within these Iverni, the various groups had different names, most prominent being the Vinducati, Soborgii, Darinii and Uluti towards the north, the Ceuleni and Aucii on the east coast, the Gamarnates in the west, and the Autinii and Veldobri in the south.

A strong challenge to the Iverni soon presented

itself in the form of an amalgam of peoples in the broad area of the southern midlands, headed by a band of warriors belonging to the Brigantes of central Britain who had crossed the Irish Sea. The group became known as Leiquni ('casters'), a name which was reinterpreted as Lagini ('lance-men'). These Lagini seem to have coalesced at an early date with another group of incomers called Gaiso-lingi ('javelin-jumpers'), and together they extended their power over most of the south-eastern quarter of Ireland.

In the first century AD, new groups were arriving from Britain, escaping from the devastation caused by the Roman legions. These, such as the Dumnonii and Coriondi, joined with the Lagini, who began to threaten

Above: The Petrie Crown, an example of early Irish Celtic metalworking.

Left: Dún Eoghanachta, a massive ring fort on the island of Inishmore. Probably built in the fifth century, the fort takes it name from the Eoghanacht people who ruled most of Munster at this time.

Above: St. Patrick makes his way to the ritual centre of Tara some time in the fifth century.

the Ivernian kingdom of the north midlands. There are several indications that the prestigious ritual centre of Tara was seized from the Iverni by the Lagini in or about the second century. Meanwhile, in the south another group—with origins in south-west Britain or in Brittany—was building up a strong power-base. This was the Venii, who divided into two sections. One of these sections remained in the south, winning more and more territory from the Ivernian tribes there; while the other section moved northwards along the west bank of the Shannon and began to threaten the Lagini. By the early fifth century, they had crossed the Shannon and seized Tara from the Lagini, whom they pushed southwards beyond the river Boyne. Further migrations into Ireland were caused by the Roman campaigns against the north of Britain in the second and third centuries. The Celtic and Celticised peoples of that area were called Priteni ('painters'), which name was changed to Cruithni in Ireland. Reaching Ireland, these migrants settled in scattered groups in the north-east and on both sides of the Shannon.

From all of these groups are descended the Gaelic people of Ireland, with names developing into specifically Irish forms. For instance, the name of the country

Éveriu became Ériu and later still Éire, while the Iverni became Érainn. Strong groups among them kept their separate designations—especially the Uluti ('bearded men'), who became Ulaidh. For their part, the Lagini became Laighin, and the Cruithni became Cruithin. The Venii became Féni, with their southern section known as Eoghanacht and their northern section known as Connachta. This latter in time became the most powerful of all Irish septs, controlling the Boyne valley, as well as the large area west of the Shannon which still retains their name.

Below: Dry stone cells constructed by monks on the island of Skellig Michael some time in the sixth century are perfectly preserved.

Ireland came to be considered as naturally divided into five parts, each part called a 'fifth' (cúige)—Ulaidh in the north; Connachta in the west; Midhe ('centre') comprising the north midland plain; Laighin in the south-east; and Mumhain ('the nurturing' i.e. domain of the land-goddess) in the south. Later in English these were known respectively as Ulster, Connacht, Meath, Leinster and Munster. Midhe as a provincial unit ceased to exist in the Middle Ages, and its territory is in fact part of the modern increased province of Leinster. This accounts for the four historic provinces of Ireland. In modern Irish, of course, the Irish people themselves are called Gaeil or Éireannaigh, and the inhabitants of the four provinces are called

Above: A map of 1700 showing the Irish provinces of Ulster, Munster, Leinster and Connacht before the partition of Ireland.

respectively Ultaigh, Connachtaigh, Laighnigh and Muimhnigh.

Many Irish septs are still identifiable in the mediaeval period as descendants of the Érainn, Laighin, Connachta and Eoghanacht, and a lesser number of the Cruithin. These population groups had, however, developed into loose federations of kingdoms, ruled by strong extended families called *cineál* ('septs'), each of which had a traditional septal name. A leader was referred to by his own personal name, and for clarity he was described as son of his named father. These simple patronymics gave way in the tenth and 11th centuries to habitual surnames of the type we now have. The septal names gradually came to be identified more with the territories inhabited by the septs than with the septs themselves.

In the year 795, the first Norse raiders appeared off the Irish coast, and within a generation or two they had progressed from being raiders to forming settlements. They set up some kingdoms inland, but those established by them on the sea-ports were more enduring. Despite the ebb and flow of almost incessant war in opposition to, and in alliance with different Irish septs, they remained an important force, with the Norse language being spoken in their settlements for several centuries. A considerable number of Irish surnames derive from the Norsemen, either by direct descent or by the interchange of culture.

The Normans, far-out cousins of the Irish Norsemen, conquered Ireland in the late 12th century, bringing with them Welsh, English, French and Flemish supporters. Within a century or two English became the dominant language among these settlers, but many of the chief Norman families in Ireland became strongly Gaelicised. They introduced a system of dividing the country into baronies, generally giving these baronies the names of the old septal territories. A large number of Irish surnames are of Norman extraction.

Above: Carving of a Norse ship.

The system of dividing Ireland into counties, each county comprising several baronies, dates from the reign of Queen Elizabeth I. Her successor, King James I, oversaw the Ulster Plantation, which brought in large numbers of settlers speaking Scottish Lallan, Scottish Gaelic and English. With the strengthening of rule from London, the English language gradually spread throughout the whole country and, with the widespread confiscation of land and its bestowal on settlers, many specifically English names entered the country. Most of these first names and some of the surnames developed Irish forms, but the contrary process was

Left: Norman ruins at sunset in Ballybunion, Co. Kerry.

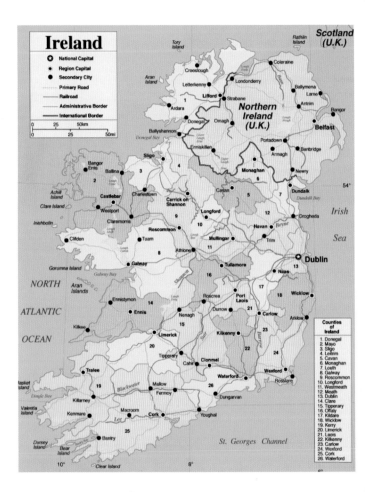

much stronger. Official versions of place-names were imposed in English, and anglicised forms of native Irish names were developed. It should be stressed that these anglicised forms, most prevalent in usage nowadays, are nearly all meaningless and give little indication of their derivation.

In Ireland there are numerous surnames of English, Scottish, Welsh, French, and other provenance. The histories of all these merit interest stretching beyond Ireland to their respective countries of origin. For general accounts of Irish surnames, see Edward MacLysaght, *Irish Families* (1957), *More Irish Families* (Dublin, 1960), *Supplement to Irish Families* (1964), and especially his *Surnames of Ireland* (1973). The last work contains a fine bibliography, as does Brian de Breffny, *Bibliography of Irish Family History and Genealogy* (1974). Further detail can be found in the many county and diocesan histories, as well as in learned journals which deal with historical and genealogical matters.

Argyle a muckle Scotch Knau in gude faith Sir.

Above: Satirical portrayal of Scottish Presbyterians who settled in Ulster during the 17th century.

Opposite page: A map of the modern counties of Ireland. The system of dividing Ireland into counties dates from the reign of Elizabeth I.

Left: A detail of the arms of the O'Malley family on the altar tomb in Clare Abbey.

GENEALOGY

IRELAND'S DRAMATIC

HISTORY, LIKE ALL HISTORY,

IS COMPOSED OF COUNTLESS

INDIVIDUAL FAMILY

HISTORIES, EACH UNIQUE.

GENEALOGY

As we have shown, the Irish—like other nationalities—are in reality a worthy mixture of many different peoples. Genealogy can give but a tiny insight into our background, for the available information tends to be uneven, focusing mostly on people of social standing. The study of genealogy is an enjoyable pastime, but it should not involve any exclusiveness, for our dignity depends not on our descent but on our common humanity and individual personalities.

The first step in researching one's genealogy is to talk to relatives and friends, particularly elderly ones, and to note down all the information they have about the family tree. This ought to trace the tree back through two generations at least.

Documents pertaining to the household can also be of help, no matter how ephemeral they may seem. A journey to the local library comes next to see if members of the family are mentioned in any documents or publications there. One can also consult inscriptions on graveyard headstones where family members are known to be buried. Lists of old gravestone inscriptions for many counties are kept in the Genealogical Office (GO) and the National Archives of Ireland, Dublin (NAI), and others are published in local journals.

Above: Tracing your family tree is an enjoyable pastime. The first step is to talk to elderly relatives and friends, and note down any information they can offer.
Previous pages: The Book of the Boyles, showing the descent of the earls of Cork and Orrery.

Several parts of Ireland now have local heritage centres, in which copies and indexes of many records, as well as published works, are kept. Information in these centres will have been selected from the range of surviving sources for the study of Irish genealogy, and are listed here in general chronological order.

Earliest in date are the septal pedigrees—compiled at various periods from the sixth century AD to the Middle Ages. The prehistoric origins in these pedigrees are partly fanciful, but otherwise they provide invaluable material. The texts have been assembled by Michael A. O'Brien in *Corpus Genealogiarum Hiberniae* (1962). Several mediaeval and post-mediaeval genealogies have been edited and compiled by John O'Donovan —for whose work see R. I. Best, *Bibliography of Irish Philology and of Printed Irish Literature*, vol. 1 (1913), 295. Traditional pedigrees of various Irish septs are also given in editions such as Toirdhealbhach Ó Raithbheartaigh, *Genealogical Tracts* (1932); and Tadhg Ó Donnchadha, *An Leabhar Muimhneach* (1940). An edition by Nollaig Ó Muraile is forthcoming of the *Book of Genealogies* compiled from old sources by the 17th-century scholar, Dubhaltach Mac Fir Bhisigh.

A large number of pedigrees, compiled since the 16th century, are in GO. For the early 17th century, the

Above: Consulting the inscriptions of gravestones where family members are known to be buried can be a fruitful exercise in drawing up the family tree.

Left: The reading room of the National Library of Ireland, Dublin.

Calendar of Irish Patent Rolls of James I (published by IMC in 1966) gives the names of persons to whom land was granted by that king. For 1612–13, there is a list of 'Undertakers' i.e. English and Scottish landlords who were granted land in the Ulster Plantation (published in *The Historical Manuscripts Commission Reports*, vol. 4). For 1630 and 1642, the Muster Rolls name large landlords in Ulster and able-bodied men on whom they could call to fight (copies are in the NLI and the Public Record Office of Northern Ireland, Belfast [PRONI]).

For 1641 and 1681 there are the *Books of Survey and Distribution* i.e. an English Government list of land ownership for distribution after confiscation. This material—from which the results from County Meath are lacking—is in NAI, with microfilm copies in NLI

Below: The start of the official pedigree of the O'Neills, housed at the Genealogical Office in Dublin.

and transcripts in the Royal Irish Academy, Dublin (RIA). The books for Counties Roscommon, Mayo, Galway and Clare have been published by the Irish Manuscripts Commission (IMC). For 1641 to 1698, *Lists of Outlaws* consist of over 6,000 names of people outlawed whose lands were confiscated—microfilm copies of an abstract are in NLI.

For 1654, the *Civil Survey of Ireland* (published by IMC in 3 volumes in 1931), covers Counties Tipperary, Limerick, Waterford, Meath, Donegal and Derry, with incomplete entries for Counties Kerry, Dublin, Kildare, Wexford and Tyrone. It lists the landlords of each townland and their predecessors in 1641. For 1654, the *Down Survey* gives names of landowners and their religion (published by the Irish Archaeological Society in 1851). For 1659, there is a census of most counties, compiled by Sir William Petty (published by IMC in 1931, ed. Seamus Pender, *The Census of Ireland*).

For 1662 to 1666 Subsidy Rolls are principally concerned with Ulster. They list the nobility, clergy and laity who paid grants in aid to King Charles II. Some of these rolls are in NAI and PRONI, with transcripts in the Representative Church Body Library, Dublin (RCBL). For 1664 to 1666, Hearth Money Rolls give the name of each householder whose dwelling had a hearth. Copies of various of these are in GO, NAI, NLI, PRONI and RCBL.

For 1689 and 1690, information on Irish Jacobites is given by John D'Alton in *Illustrations Historical and Genealogical of King James II's Irish Army List* (published in 1689, and reissued in 1861); and in ed. C. E. Lart, *The Pedigrees and Papers of James Terry 1690–1725* (1938). For 1703, the Convert Rolls list Roman Catholics who changed their religion to the Church of

Above: A page from the Book of the Boyles, with the various families represented heraldically.

Ireland (published in IMC Reports in 1981, ed. Eileen O'Byrne). For 1740, there is a list of Protestant householders in several Ulster counties available in GO.

A large number of legal deeds, from 1708 onwards, are registered with indexes in the Registry of Deeds, Dublin (RD). Newspapers began in Ireland in the early 18th century. Good collections of them are held in NLI. Names and addresses of persons engaged in business are in the various directories which were published from the mid 18th century onwards. The best collections of these directories are in NAI and NLI.

Only people of substance made wills, but much information can be gleaned from them. A huge collection of wills, dating from 1536 to 1900, was destroyed in a fire in the Public Record Office of Ireland, Dublin (PROI) in 1922, but copies, abstracts, or indexes of over 60 per cent of them survive in NAI. There are also substantial holdings in GO, NLI and PRONI. Some of the material has been published in journals, and by Sir Arthur Vicars, *Index to the Prerogative Wills of Ireland 1536-1810* (Dublin, 1897).

There are fragments of Roman Catholic parish records dating from the late 17th century, but the first appreciable collections are much later —beginning variously in the later 18th century and the 19th century. They contain details of baptisms and of marriages. Microfilm copies of almost all this material are in NLI, but diocesan permission is required to consult some of it. Church of Ireland (Protestant) registers began earlier—some as early as the mid 17th century. Most of its parish registers up to 1871 were destroyed by

Below: Only people of substance made wills, but much information can be gleaned from them.

Last Will and Testament

Being of sound mind and body, I do hereby declare this to be my last will and testame...

Above: Birth certificates are housed at the General Register Office in Dublin.

fire in the PROI in 1922, but RCBL—where the Church of Ireland archives are preserved—has worked admirably to restore the losses. Some records of Presbyterian congregations also date to the 17th century, but registers were not comprehensively undertaken until the 19th century. Microfilms of most of these registers from Northern Ireland until 1900 are in PRONI, whereas most from the rest of Ireland are in local custody. Copies of Methodist and Quaker records are also kept in PRONI. Good lists for clergymen of all denominations are on microfilm in NLI, some of them reaching back to the early 18th century.

For 1775–76, there is a list of Roman Catholics from various counties who took the Oath of Allegiance to the king of England (published in the *59th Report of the Deputy Keeper* of PROI). For 1778–93, Catholic Qualification Rolls list other Roman Catholics who took the Oath. An index to it—containing names, occupations, dates and places—survives in NAI.

For 1795, the Charter Trust Fund Marriage Certificates in NAI list Protestant labourers in north Leinster and County Cavan who were given small gratuities on marriage. For 1796, a Spinning Wheel Entitlement gives by district the names of persons—almost 60,000 in all, mostly in Ulster—who received free spinning wheels through a government scheme to encourage the linen trade. Indexes to the list are in NAI and PRONI. Details from two interesting local census survive—one from Elphin Diocese in 1749 (in NAI); and one for the town of Carrick-on-Suir in 1799 (microfilm copy in NLI).

Above: For 1796 a Spinning-Wheel Entitlement gives the names of persons who received spinning wheels as part of a government scheme.

For 1823 to 1838, the Tithe Applotment Books, and related material for all Ireland, specify the amount of money to be paid by each landholder to the Church of Ireland. Poor people also had to pay these tithes. The originals are in NAI; with microfilm copies in NLI and (for the nine Ulster counties) in PRONI. For 1848 to 1864, the Valuation of Ireland was carried out under the direction of Richard Griffith (published at the time by the General Valuation Office, Dublin [GVO], as *The Valuation of Ireland*). Householders' names are listed by

Below: Irish peasantry. Tithes fell most heavily on the poor.

county, barony, parish and townland. The surnames which occur in this source and in the Tithe Applotments are arranged by parish in a combined index, copies of which are in NLI, NAI, PRONI and GO. Less extensive revaluation books, covering the period down to 1929, are in GVO and PRONI. From 1837 to 1896, the

Incumbered Estate Records, with details concerning the estates of bankrupt landlords, are preserved in NLI. For 1876, *Landowners in Ireland* (published officially in London in 1876) gives a list of the 32,614 persons—identified by province and county—who owned land exceeding an acre in that year.

Of great value are the National School Records for 1831 to 1921, which give the name, age and religion of each pupil, as well as the parents' address and occupation. PRONI has most of these registers for the six northern counties, but for the other 26 counties the school records are still kept locally. From 1838 to 1848, the Poor Law Records give details of inmates of workhouses and infirmaries—parts survive and are available in NAI, PRONI and county libraries. With the introduction of the Old Age Pension scheme in 1908, much information was assembled concerning the claimants and their families—these records are preserved in NAI and PRONI. Much more comprehensively, the General Register Office, Dublin (GRO) has

Below: Irish schoolgirls in the 1890s. National school records are of great value in tracing your genealogy.

records of all births, marriages, and deaths, from 1864 for all counties up to 1921, and for the 26 counties of the Republic thereafter. For the six northern counties after 1921, these records are held in The Register General, Belfast (RG).

There are also other lists and valuations, variously kept in GO, NAI, NLI, PRONI, TCD and other locations. These include local lists of freeholders compiled from the 17th century onwards. From the same period are miscellaneous voters' lists and poll-tax books. More comprehensive are the lists of, and files on, state prisoners and convicted persons, covering the period 1788 to 1868, in the State Paper Office, Dublin (SPO). Militia and army lists from 1750 onwards are preserved variously in GO, NLI, PRONI and the Public Record Office at Kew in Surrey, England. Details of policemen for all of Ireland, from 1816 to 1922, are kept in microfiche copies in NAI and PRONI.

The most efficient method of tracing relatives would be from census reports; however, the material available is very unsatisfactory. A full census of Ireland was taken every ten years from 1821 to 1911, but only

Above: A 19th-century workhouse. Poor Law records can provide details of inmates of workhouses between 1838 and 1848.

Right: A cartoon satirising the policies which caused large numbers of people to emigrate from Ireland.

Left: A sketch of a man taking a census around 1870. A full census of Ireland was taken every ten years from 1821 to 1911, but only fragments of these records remain.

fragments of these records remain. Now in NAI, they are as follows: 1821 (partially for Counties Cavan, Fermanagh, Galway, Meath and Offaly); 1831 (partially for County Derry); 1841 (Killeshandra in County Cavan only); 1851 (partial, mostly from County Antrim). In addition, some transcripts and abstracts made from the original 1841 to 1891 returns have been found. This means that the earliest comprehensive returns which survive come from the census taken in 1901 and 1911, kept in NAI. Copies of the 1901 returns for the six counties of Northern Ireland are also available at PRONI. No census was taken in 1921, and subsequent census are subject to a 100-year closure.

Derived from several of the above-mentioned sources is the Irish section of the *International Genealogical Index*, compiled by the Church of Jesus Christ of Latter-Day Saints (CLDS) and available in their major repositries. For detailed information on sources and how to consult them, see John Grenham, *Tracing Your Irish Ancestors* (Dublin, 1999).

THE WALSHES

SEANCHAS BREATNACH

THE MOTTO OF THESE FAMILIES IS, IN LATIN, *MELIORA SPERO* ('FOR BETTER THINGS I HOPE!'). THE NAME WAS USED TO DENOTE VARIOUS INDIVIDUALS WHO CAME TO IRELAND WITH THE NORMAN INVASION. ALTHOUGH THE WALSHES ARE ACCORDINGLY OF VARYING DESCENT, BEARERS OF THE SURNAME HAVE SHOWN REMARKABLE EMPATHY WITH EACH OTHER DOWN THROUGH THE CENTURIES.

CELTIC CONNECTIONS

England was rapidly taken over by the Normans after the Battle of Hastings in 1066, but the conquest of Wales was more difficult. Real progress was made only after the king of Dyfed, Rhys ap Tewdwr, was slain in 1090. Most of south Wales fell to the invaders soon after, and in 1097 Pembroke Castle was bestowed by the English king, William Rufus, on a Norman knight called Gerald of Windsor. The Welsh rebelled again in 1136, and it took some years for the Normans to regain control, but already a mixed population of Welsh and Normans was growing up, and several of the Norman leaders too had Welsh blood in their veins.

Particularly evident was the role of Nesta, daughter of Rhys ap Tewdwr. Through her affair with King Henry I of England, brother and successor of William Rufus, she became the mother of Henry FitzHenry. By her marriage to Gerald of Windsor she became the mother of William of Carew, Maurice FitzGerald, Bishop David of St David's, and Angharet who married William de Bari. Finally, by another liaison with Stephen of Cardigan, she became the mother of Robert FitzStephen. Thus, some of the most powerful families engaged in the Norman conquest of Ireland—the Carews, FitzGeralds, and Barrys—were of the direct line of the Welsh king of Dyfed. It should be added that the Marshalls and Vescis are descended from Raymond le Gros, son of William of Carew, and that the Condons are descended from Raymond's sister; while the Cogans are descended from Robert FitzStephen.

Surnames had not yet become standardised in the

Left: Brecon Beacons National Park in south Wales. Most of south Wales fell to Norman invaders by the end of the 11th century, leading to the growth of a population with mixed Norman and Welsh blood.

Above: Pembroke Castle, instrumental to Norman power in south-west Wales, occupied a strategic position on a major routeway.

12th century, and several of the Norman incomers were known by their specific place of origin rather than by patronymics. In several cases, since most of them came from Wales, this was the general place of origin to which reference was made. Thus many individual Normans arriving in Ireland were known simply by their first names plus a soubriquet such as Waleis, Waleys, or Waley. This was rendered by the mediaeval writers in Latin as Wallia, Wallenis, Britannicus, or Cambrensis, leaving no doubt as to its meaning—simply 'Welshman'. It is likely that these were to some degree of Welsh descent, as it was normal for the Saxons and Normans to refer to neighbouring peoples of Celtic origin—be they in the Scottish borderland, in Wales, in Cornwall, or even in Brittany—as 'Welsh', meaning 'wild people'. Regarding the use of the term for some Normans in Ireland, it has been argued that some of these derived from Owain Gwynedd, a celebrated prince of north Wales, and from his brother, Cadwalader.

The differing origins of the 'Welshmen' in Norman Ireland is reflected by the fact that early on the name split into two variants. Some came to be generally referred to as 'de Waleis', which became in time Wallace

or Wallis, or in Irish de Bhailís. Families for whom this solidified into a surname spread to parts of Counties Cork, Limerick, and Galway, in all of which areas they are still to be found. It is also frequent as a surname in Ulster, where it is of Scottish origin. The ancient Britons of the Celtic kingdom of Strathclyde were called by the Normans—in the usual manner—'Waleis', thus giving rise to the surname in that area. William Wallace, the celebrated Scottish hero, (1272–1305) was of this people.

By far the greater number of the 'people from Wales', however, were referred to individually as 'le Waleis', and this became Walsh or Walshe, and in

Left: Incised effigy from a tomb slab at Jerpoint Abbey, Co. Kilkenny, depicts the arrival of the Normans in Ireland.

Right: The celebrated Scottish hero William Wallace. The ancient Britons of the Celtic kingdom of Strathclyde were called 'Waleis' by the Normans, thus giving rise to the surname of Wallace in this area.

Below: Killary Harbour, Co. Galway. The Wallace or Wallis variant of the Walsh name is common in this county, as well as parts of Counties Cork and Limerick.

Irish Breatnach or Breathnach (the ordinary term for a Welshman). This surname is nowadays very common and found in several counties. Its pronunciation is usually 'Welsh', but in north Leinster and Ulster it can be 'Wolsh'. The Irish form is pronounced according to usual dialectal variation—with the stress on the initial syllable as 'bra-na' in Ulster and 'bra-nugh' in Leinster and Connacht; but with stress on the second syllable in Munster, 'bri-nogh'. From the Irish form of the name comes a variant sometimes found in English, Brannagh.

TRADITIONS OF THE EARLY WALSHES

The first mention of the appellation in Ireland concerns the young brothers Philip and David, both termed 'le Waleis'. The official records show that these were closely allied with the family of William of Carew (d.1173), son of Gerald of Windsor and Nesta. They seem, indeed, to have come to Ireland with William's famous son, Raymond le Gros, in 1170. Claims that they were nephews of Raymond are difficult to prove, but they would appear to have been related to him in some way. They may have been in reality children of a Welshman who married a relative of Raymond's father, for a contemporary source, the writer Giraldus 'Cambrensis' de Bari, states that they were not pure Welsh by blood.

A genealogy of a later date, which gives Walsh and Wallis as alternative forms of their names, has David and Philip as nephews of the most powerful of the Norman invaders of Ireland, Richard de Clare ('Strongbow'), earl of Pembroke. Here it is claimed that they came from Cornwall but that they were 'descended from the famous David, king of Wales'. By this latter may be meant the north Welsh king David, nephew of Cadwalader. This derivation is much confused, however. A cousin of Strongbow, Alicia de Clare, did indeed marry Cadwalader, and through their son, Cadogan, this couple would appear to have been ancestors of some later families called 'Walsh' in Ireland.

Below: The seal of Strongbow, displaying typical Anglo-Norman pride in their military prowess.

Above: The reputed tomb of Strongbow who died in 1176, in Christchurch Cathedral, Dublin.

At any rate, Philip le Waleis was in Raymond's force which in 1173 invaded the territory in west Waterford of Diarmaid Mac Cárthaigh, king of Desmond (south Munster). They were bringing some of the plunder by sea from Dungarvan to their headquarters in Waterford, when they were attacked by the fleet of the Danes from Cork who were loyal to Diarmaid. During the sea-battle, it is reported that the commander of the Cork fleet, Gilbert Thorgilsson, was slain in single combat by Philip; and one account claims that Philip actually leapt onto the deck of his rival's boat before killing him with his sword.

Again, in 1175, Raymond and his cousin Miler FitzHenry, grandson of King Henry I, brought a force to attack Limerick, the headquarters of Domhnall Ó Briain, king of Thomond (north Munster). The river Shannon was in flood, and it seemed impossible to reach the walls of the town. Young David le Waleis spurred his horse into the water and, though almost drowned, made his way across. Seeing this, Miler FitzHenry and the others were encouraged to follow, and though they did not take Limerick on that occasion, the bravery of David was much applauded.

Soon after, Diarmaid Mac Cárthaigh was imprisoned by his own son, Cormac, who wished to take the Desmond kingdom for himself. Diarmaid appealed for assistance to Raymond le Gros. When Raymond helped him to regain his position, Diarmaid gave lands to his benefactor in County Kerry. As part of the new rapprochement, Raymond's son, Richard, married the daughter of Mac Cárthaigh; while Máire, daughter of a kinsman of Mac Cárthaigh, was given in marriage to David le Waleis. David's brother, Philip, married another Desmond noblewoman and was given much land with her in the Comeragh mountains in County Waterford. In 1199, land was granted by King John in

Below: Thomond Bridge over the Shannon river and King John's Castle in Limerick. In 1175, Raymond and his cousin Miler FitzHenry, grandson of King Henry I, brought a force to attack Limerick.

Above: The Comeragh mountains, Co. Waterford. Philip le Waleis, who married a Desmond noblewoman, was given much land in this area.

south County Cork to Philip's son, Maurice. By 1207 settlements were being made by 'Walshes' as far west as County Kerry—relatives of David under the patronage of Miler FitzHenry near Castleisland; and sons of Philip west of Killarney, perhaps under the patronage of Raymond's son, Richard de Carew.

Some time later, David received a grant of land from King Henry II at Carrickmines in south County Dublin. The authority and the associates of these Walshes having penetrated into remote parts of the south, the opportunity to expand so near to the fountain-head of power in Ireland was not missed. Before long, David and his descendants owned extensive properties in south Dublin and adjacent areas. A particularly

Right: King Henry II of England at Waterford.

strong settlement was made in south County Kildare, which became known as Baile Breatnach (Brannockstown, near Ballimore Eustace). Philip, probably a son of David, had lands at Bray in County Wicklow and Lusk in County Dublin in 1219; Gilbert le Waleis had property in Dún Laoghaire and Howth, both in County Dublin, in the middle of the century; and

Above: The ruins of Howth Abbey. Gilbert le Waleis had property in this area in the mid 1300s.

around 1300 Richard and Thomas le Waleis had property at Athgoe, Co. Dublin. Henry le Waleis was keeper of Dublin Castle in 1294, and William was sheriff of Dublin in 1331 and Robert in 1360.

A fine castle at Carrickmines was intended by the Anglo-Normans as a bulwark against the Gaelic septs of Wicklow, especially the O'Byrnes and O'Tooles, who repeatedly tried to regain territory which had been taken from the Irish. So, in 1371, an army had to be rushed from Dublin to Carrickmines when the castle was being assailed by the O'Byrnes. At the beginning of the 15th century, Henry of Carrickmines was 'captayne of the Walshe men', and in 1417 Maurice and William Walsh were to the fore in the Anglo-Norman alliance against the native Wicklow septs. Having spread westwards into Counties Kildare and Laois, these Walshes worked closely with the powerful earls of Kildare, who as FitzGeralds were relatives of theirs, and from there spread further afield—into Meath and even further north to parts of County Down.

Right: County Kildare. In 1417 Maurice and William Walsh were to the fore of an Anglo-Norman alliance against the native Wicklow septs. Having spread westwards into Counties Kildare and Laois, these Walshes worked closely with the powerful earls of Kildare, spreading further afield into Meath and even County Down.

A peculiar instance of the adoption of the name Walsh is evidenced by the introduction of Norman families into Tirawley in County Mayo in or about 1237. These were introduced by Richard de Carew as part of an attempted Norman plantation of Connacht. They moved there from County Cork, along with the Barrett family, and their tradition was that these two groups took their names from two brothers who led the settlers—one of them called Walynus and the other Beraud.

Meanwhile, in the original area of the Norman invasion in south Leinster, others bearing the name were also meeting with success. One of the first settlers in

Wexford was one Walter Howell, whose holding is reported at Old Ross in or about the year 1180. He was a son of Howell or Haylen, and it is interesting that this was a variant of the Welsh name Hywel. One tradition is that Howell was a younger son of the prolific Princess Nesta, while another makes him somewhat younger by claiming that he was a son of Philip le Waleis. These traditions seem to be of later invention, but the real Howell probably did have some connection with that extended family.

The descendants of Walter Howell were not slow to expand, and the Howell who held Carrickbyrne, further south in County Wexford, in 1247 was either his son or his grandson. This family also excelled at business and trade—one Griffen le Waleis of Old Ross is listed as a leading entrepreneur in the year 1280. He was provost of Old Ross until his death in 1288, after which he was succeeded in that office by his son, Henry. From this time on, there is repeated mention of the trading and shipping activities of these Walshes, especially centred on the fine residence which they built on the Great Island, on the eastern side of

Above: The Barrett family coat of arms. This Norman family were introduced to Tirawley, Co. Mayo along with the Walshes around 1237 as part of an attempted Norman plantation of Connacht.
Below: Waterford city and harbour, where the Walshes had successful shipping and trading interests.

Above: Kells Priory, Co. Kilkenny. Stephen Howell got possession of land in this area which had previosly belonged to Geoffrey FitzRobert.

Waterford harbour. Some of them in fact settled in Waterford city itself, becoming successful merchants there and having their residence at Ballygunner.

Stephen Howell had Carrickbyrne in 1286 and, soon after, he got possession of land near Kells in County Kilkenny, land which had previously belonged to Geoffrey FitzRobert, brother-in-law of Raymond le Gros. He also acquired land, in the same area, which had belonged to Raymond's brother, Griffen de Carew. His initial residence in the area seems to have been at Sean-Chathair (Oldcourt) in Templeorum, but his son and successor—yet another Howell—built a new residence, Castle Howell (later Castlehale), a few kilometres further north in Rossanarra townland near Kilmoganny. From this Howell are descended *Breatnaigh an tSléibhe*, 'the Walshes of the mountain', this 'mountain' being a designation for the hilly country between the Suir and the Nore in south Kilkenny. They had no fewer than 18 castles in that area. It is interesting to note that these Kilkenny Walshes continued to keep close contact with their Wexford cousins.

Meanwhile, in west Waterford, the family of Philip le Waleis was also growing richer. William, son of Philip, added to his Comeragh property, extending it to the Kilkenny-Tipperary border and beyond. These additional lands were granted by the Norman ruler, Thomas FitzAntony, who was established there in 1215 by the powerful William Marshall, son-in-law and heir of Strongbow. FitzAntony fell victim to the quarrel between King Henry III and Marshall's son, Richard, in 1234, but his daughter married John FitzGerald, lord of Shanid in County Limerick, who—like all his Geraldine family—was partial to the Walshes.

In 1261, the MacCarthys scored a resounding victory over the FitzGeralds in the Battle of Callan, in which John and his son Maurice fell. A widespread native resurgence followed, but in 1280 Gilbert le Waleis, a relative of the Comeragh Walshes, who had land on the Waterford side of the river Blackwater, joined an alliance with the Barrys to restore the fortunes of the Geraldines. These efforts were successful. Thomas FitzGerald, grandson of John, retook most of the conquered lands from the MacCarthys, thus laying the foundation for that family's great earldom in the south—his son Maurice FitzGerald was to become the first earl of Desmond.

Out of gratitude for the assistance rendered,

Above: King Henry III of England.

Thomas FitzGerald made Gilbert le Waleis sheriff of Cork and bestowed a large estate on him near Midleton, which became known as Baile an Bhreatnaigh (Walshtown). Although loyal to the English interest, Gilbert had a friendly attitude to the native Irish, and indeed many of the co-bearers of his surname were growing greatly Gaelicised at this time.

The Butlers were by now quickly becoming the most powerful Anglo-Norman family in all of south Leinster, and in 1315 they got the whole barony of Iverk from the last Geraldine lord in County Kilkenny, Roger FitzDavid, descendant of Bishop David of Wales. Much of these lands were let by the Butlers to the Walshes from nearby Castle Howell, who—as we have seen—may have been relatives of the FitzDavids. A

Below: Jerpoint Abbey, Co. Kilkenny. Richard Walsh made a generous grant of land to the abbey in 1446. Richard's son, Edmund, was buried here in 1476.

great-grandson of Howell Walsh, called Geoffrey, was in possession of Castle Howell in 1374. His son, Richard Walsh, was appointed keeper of the peace for County Kilkenny in 1410, and in 1446 Richard made a generous grant of lands to Jerpoint Abbey. Richard's son, Edmund, married a lady of the Butlers, Johanna, and was buried at Jerpoint in 1476.

Life was not uneventful for the Walshes in those years. In 1310 one Robert le Waleis of Waterford was accused of murder and of 'being a robber and harbouring robbers'. More respectable was Richard le Waleis of County Tipperary, one of 14 of the principal men of

Above: Roger Mortimer, earl of March, favourite of Queen Isabella and one of Edward II's disaffected nobles who forced Edward to abdicate in favour of his son, the future Edward III. In 1330 Mortimer was proclaimed an outlaw by Edward III.

Ireland whom King Edward III called upon in 1330 to apprehend the usurper of the English throne, Roger Mortimer, should Mortimer land in Ireland. In 1421, King Henry V appointed as assessor for Kildare one Philip Walsh and for Tipperary one John Walsh of Rathronan, just north of Clonmel. A descendant of the latter, James Walsh, petitioned against the exactions of Pierce Rua Butler, earl of Ormond, in 1542 . This shows a split in loyalties in the family, for the earl of Ormond was in times of crisis invariably supported by the Kilkenny Walshes.

TRAGIC TIMES IN IRELAND

The Walshes of Kilkenny remained staunch in their support of the Butlers, even in the scheming of that family to destroy the Geraldine earls of Kildare and Desmond. By contrast, the Kildare Walshes were strong supporters of the earls of Kildare. The branch of these which resided at Ticroghan (near

Right: Lord Thomas FitzGerald renounces his allegiance to Henry VIII. The Walshes who resided at Ticroghan, Co. Meath, took part in this rebellion.

Clonard in County Meath) were in fact the official standard-bearers of the Kildares, and took part in the rebellion of Silken Thomas FitzGerald in 1534–35. Fr. Richard Walsh went to Spain to implore assistance for Silken Thomas from the emperor Charles V. After the failure of the rebellion, another priest, Fr. Robert Walsh, showed remarkable courage and dexterity in spiriting away the boy-heir to the Kildare earldom to safety on the Continent.

The rebellion showed how precarious the position of these Walshes was. Although provoked by the English authorities to 'inhabit upon the O'Tooles', they in fact developed friendship with these and other neighbouring Gaelic septs. In the year 1593, Henry Walsh of Shanganagh and Pierce Walsh of Kilgobbin, in south County Dublin, were witnesses to the marriage bond between a famous couple, Fiacha Mac Aodha Ó Broin and Róis Ní Thuathail, the two leading rebel figures of the O'Byrne and O'Toole clans. Pierce was an officer controlling a troop in the English service, but he led his men out of a battle against the O'Tooles in 1599. For this, he was executed by the English, along with every tenth man of his soldiers.

A very different role was played by Sir Nicholas Walsh of Piltown in County Kilkenny, one of the principal actors in the campaign against the last true earl of Desmond, Gerald FitzGerald. Sir Nicholas became Justice of Munster in 1571, in which office he proved

Left: Gerald FitzGerald, 15th earl of Desmond, is killed by a small group of soldiers in 1583.

Right: Youghal. The Walshes of County Cork who had supported Gerald FitzGerald, earl of Desmond, had all their lands in this area taken from them, and given to the Queen's favourite, Sir Walter Raleigh.

himself an ardent opportunist and earned the nickname 'the Great Dissimulator'. With the fall of the earl of Desmond in 1583, those Walshes who supported him lost out—the Walshes of County Cork, for example, had all their lands around Youghal taken from them and given to the Queen's favourite, Sir Walter Raleigh.

Despite all their efforts, tragedy lay in store too for the Walshes of Kilkenny. Robert, son of Edmund, died in 1501, and was succeeded by his son, Walter, who was known as 'chief captain of his nation'. These Kilkennymen liked proud titles, for the head of the family was also known as an *Breatnach Mór* ('the Great Walsh') and, with a view to noble descent, as *an tOidhre Breatnach* ('the Heir Walsh'). Walter married Katherine Butler, but according to folklore he encountered difficulties from another Butler lady—the celebrated Margaret FitzGerald, countess of Ormond and wife of the earl, Pierce Rua Butler. It was said that Margaret was grasping and acquisitive, and when visiting Walsh at Inchicarran Castle, near Mullinavat, Co. Kilkenny, in an unguarded moment he offered her anything she wanted at table. She demanded a plateful of special morsels of meat, which morsels could only be found in a tiny part of an ox's thigh. Thus Walsh had to slaughter all his seven herds to appease her craving appetite. On another occasion, she demanded from Walsh as much land as one bottle of flax-seed might sprout in. This again was a trick, for she intended to spread the seed far and wide, but Walsh cleverly offered her the thick brushland of Coolanass, where no seed would grow.

Below: Sir Walter Raleigh, the English soldier and explorer, and favourite of Elizabeth I.

This Walter died about 1540, and was succeeded by his eldest son, Edmund, reputedly the first of the family to whom the popular title of 'lord of the mountain' was applied. Edmund died in 1550 and was succeeded by his son, Robert. Walter, son of this Robert was 'lord of the mountain' and 'chief captain of his nation' for about 50 years. He was married to Ellice, daughter of Richard Butler, Lord Mountgarret, and his household was noted for its hospitality. He died in 1619, and his grandson and successor, another Walter, took the

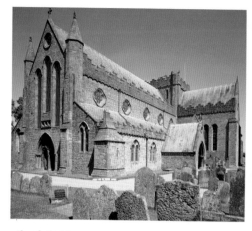

Right: The 13th-century St. Canice's Cathedral in Kilkenny. The Kilkenny Walshes suffered grievously for their opposition to Cromwell.

side of the Mountgarrets against James Butler, earl of Ormond, who commanded the English forces.

Further north, the Walshes of Dublin were also involved in the rebellion of the Irish and Anglo-Irish families, and in 1642 their castle at Carrickmines, which was under the control of Theobald and Edward Walsh, was attacked by Sir Simon Harcourt with a strong English force. Harcourt was killed in the fighting, but the castle was taken in a ferocious struggle. All

Right: James Butler, 12th earl and first duke of Ormond.

the defenders were massacred, and the castle itself was blown up.

In 1649 Sir Nicholas Walsh, son of the opportunistic Justice Nicholas, died bravely fighting against the forces of Oliver Cromwell, as also did Edmund Walsh, eldest son of Walter, 'lord of the mountain'. When Cromwell attacked Kilkenny Castle, it was defended stoutly by Governor James Walsh and Sir Walter Butler, and after fierce fighting the besiegers thought it best to allow the defending army to march away fully armed. The Kilkenny Walshes suffered grievously for their opposition to Cromwell. Castlehale was destroyed, the fighting men of the mountain were massacred and buried in a huge pit, and Walter died brokenhearted at New Ross. His surviving sons, Howell and Robert, managed to get back small portions of their estate, but when Robert perished fighting in the Irish army in the second siege of Limerick in 1691, the power of the whole family was at an end. The Walshes of Rathronan in County Tipperary, and those of County Kerry, also lost their lands in the confiscations. Some Walshes managed to cling on in Counties Dublin and Wicklow, but after the Williamite Wars the old owners withdrew to France.

Above: Kilkenny Castle, seat of the Butler family. The castle was defended stoutly by governor James Walsh and Sir Walter Butler when Cromwell attacked in 1650.

THE ILLUSTRIOUS SURNAME

For some time Walshes had been migrating to the Continent. Some of the Waterford family went to Spain while the Carrickmines branch went to Austria. The family had the longest military tradition of any of the Austro-Irish families; 11 were field marshals or generals, including Field Marshal Franz Paul Walsh (1677–1737) and George Oliver Walsh (1676–1752) who led the Austrian army against the Turks. Count Stefan Walsh (1744–1832) served with distinction against Napoleon.

Right: 18th-century Austrian soldiers. Some of the Carrickmines Walshes who migrated to Austria served with distinction in the Austrian military.

Österreicher (1728).

Left: Prince Charles Edward Stuart, better known as Bonnie Prince Charlie. A privateer at Nantes, who claimed to be one of the Walshes of Ballynacooly, was involved in transporting the prince to Scotland in 1745 to launch the rebellion.

In 1690 James Walsh from Ballynacooly in the Walsh mountains, Co. Kilkenny, conveyed James II from Ireland to France. His son, Philip (1666–1708), was a ship-builder at St. Malo and supplied vessels to the French navy. He is possibly connected to Antoine Vincent of Nantes (1703–63), a privateer who claimed to be a Walsh. He transported Prince Charles Edward Stuart to Scotland in 1745 to launch a rebellion.

Over in North America the family have continued their distinguished military and maritime service. Walsh's Regiment formed part of George Washington's Irish Brigade during the War of Revolution. During the

Right: The American pilot Kenneth Walsh. He received the Congressional Medal of Honor for a series of daring attacks in the Pacifc in 1943.

Second World War the US pilot Kenneth Walsh received the Congressional Medal of Honor, the highest US gallantry award, for a series of daring attacks in the Pacific, including a dog fight with 50 Japanese Zero fighters in 1943. US Marine Gunnery Sergeant William C. Walsh received the award posthumously for heroism on Iwo Jima in 1945.

The various families called Walsh had a great interest in genealogy, and one fanciful account which elaborates on their various traditions was drawn up by the scholar Pierce Walsh (1744–1819), of Belline in south Kilkenny. The exaggeration could go even further, and one fantastic folk tradition claims that the

Virgin Mary herself was a Walsh! This has a curious origin, for the mother of Jesus is described in the bible as of the line of David. The name of the ancient Hebrew king, of course, was also borne by St. David of Wales, and the Walsh family, being from Wales, were in a sense of the same line as this David. It would follow that, if the two Davids were confused, the Virgin Mary could be imagined as a Welshwoman, and thus she was popularly referred to as Máire Bhreatnach ('Mary Walsh')!

Left: One fantastic folk tradition claims that the Virgin Mary was herself a Walsh.

Above: Sitting Bull Council at Fort Walsh. The fort, now a national historic park, was built by James M. Walsh.

Among the leading churchmen and scholars bearing the name was Franciscan Peter Walsh (1618–88) who promoted the controversial Remonstrance as an attempt to reconcile the Catholic Church to the English Crown.

William J. Walsh (1841–1921), appointed archbishop of Dublin in 1885, played an active role in public affairs, and strongly supported the republican leadership. He was the first chancellor of the National University of Ireland.

The US mathematical genius Joseph Walsh (1859–1973) published over 300 papers and supervised 31 doctoral students at Harvard University. He developed the 'Walsh functions' that have proved indispensable tools in digital and signal processing within communications engineering. Emmett Walsh (1862–1969), born in South Carolina, became one of the world's youngest bishops at 35. Walsh University, Ohio, was named after him.

The Walsh family have also produced many politicians and officials. The Canadian mounted policeman James M. Walsh (1840–1905) was an important actor in dramatic episodes that marked the development of western Canada. He built Fort Walsh (now a national historic park) in Saskatchewan, from where he mediated with Sitting Bull and his Sioux followers who fled the United States after the Battle of the Little Bighorn (1879).

Thomas J. Walsh (1859–1933), born in Wisconsin, was a Democratic US senator from 1913 to 1933. He exposed the 1923 Teapot Dome scandal that shook the Republican administration of President W. G. Harding.

US lawyer Frank P. Walsh (1864–1939), born in Missouri, was a civil rights advocate and progressive democrat who spent his whole life fighting governments and powerful institutions. He led a private delegation of pro-Irish independence Americans who attempted to participate in the 1919 Paris Peace Conference. He was also an adviser to Irish president Éamon de Valera during the 1920s.

Left: American Democratic senator, Thomas J. Walsh, at his desk in the senate building.

Above: Maureen O'Hara and John Wayne in a publicity still for *The Quiet Man*, John Ford's film adapted from the short story by Maurice Walsh.

Right: The film director Raoul Walsh (right), and American actor Clark Gable sit together on the set of Walsh's film *The Tall Men*.

Democratic US senator David Walsh (1872–1947), born in Massachusetts, had a distinguished career as a champion of immigrants' and workers' causes. He became governor of Massachusetts in 1913 and a senator in 1918.

The family have become prominent in the arts and media. US journalist Henry C. Walsh (1863–1927) wrote a series of accounts about his adventures around the world. These included his attempt to reach the North Pole (1912), a trek through Central America, and a trip across Morocco and the Atlas Mountains (1897) by caravan. In 1925 he ventured deeper than any previous recorded descent into Endless Cavern, Virginia.

Maurice Walsh (1879–64), born in County Kerry, wrote a series of novels and short stories. 'The Quiet Man' published in *Green Rushes* (1935) was made into a celebrated film by John Ford (1952).

Raoul Walsh (1887–1980), born in New York, directed his first Hollywood picture, *The Regeneration*, in 1915. It was the first full-length gangster movie. He directed *The Thief of Baghdad* (1924), one of Douglas Fairbanks' most

popular silent movies. *What Price Glory* (1926) and *The Roaring Twenties* (1939) were two of his finest films. He also directed Errol Flyn, James Cagney, and John Wayne in various gangster, western, and war movies.

James Morgan Walsh (1897–1952) was one of Australia's most prolific popular authors, writing 58 novels under his own name and various pseudonyms. Most of his spy, crime, and adventure sagas were sold in Great Britain.

Actress Raquel Welch (1940–) was born Raquel Tejada in Chicago, Illinois. One of the most popular celebrities of the 1960s and 1970s, she appeared in a number of films including the Elvis Presley vehicle *Roustabout* (1964), and the prehistoric fantasy film *One Million Years BC* (1966).

Above: American guitarist Joe Walsh, of the hugely successful rock band The Eagles.

US guitarist Joe Walsh (1947–), born in New Jersey, joined the Eagles in 1972. They became one of the most commercially successful rock bands of the 1970s and sold 40 million albums worldwide. He is now a solo player but also joined the reunited Eagles in 1995.

Kenneth Branagh (1960–), who has a version of the Walsh surname, is one of Britain's leading actors. The Northern Irish dramatist has also directed several Royal Shakespeare Company productions and

Above: Kenneth Branagh and Emma Thomspon in a production of *Look Back in Anger*. The name Branagh is a variation of the Walsh surname.

Hollywood screenplays.

Several sporting heroes bear the name. Edmund ('Big Ed') Walsh, born in Pennsylvania, began his major league baseball career in 1902. The pitcher went on to have a 14-year major league career, mainly with Chicago's White Sox. His feat of winning 40 games and pitching 464 innings in 1908 was unsurpassed in the 20th century.

David Walsh (1889–1975), born in New Jersey, became a successful basketball coach and official. He made a significant contribution to the sport as a driving force in establishing uniformity in the application of basketball rules worldwide.

Bill Walsh (1931–), born in Los Angeles, had an outstanding career as a US football coach, especially with the San Francisco 49ers. As their head coach (1979–89) he helped them win the 1982, 1985, and 1989 Super Bowls.

Right: Bill Walsh, the outstanding American football coach.

Ollie Walsh (1937–96), born in County Kilkenny, was a legendary hurler. After a superb playing career he became a successful manager.

The legendary Jamaican cricketer Courtney Walsh (1962–) is an outstanding fast bowler. He first captained the West Indies in 1994, and in March 2000 became the highest wicket-taker in Test history.

Above: The Walsh Glacier in the St. Elias Mountains of Alaska.

Several places bear the name Walsh. North Dakota's Walsh County, created in 1881, was named after George H. Walsh (1845–1913), who was a local newspaperman and politician. Walsh Town is an agricultural district in Baca County, southeast Colorado. Walsh Glacier is a large glacier flowing from icefields in the St. Elias Mountains of Alaska and Yukon Territory. At home in Ireland, in Walshestown, Co. Down, a castle occupied by the Barrys stood for over 400 years years until it was demolished and the stones used in the building of the present Walshestown House (c. 1755–60).

The Walsh family have ventured across the globe in search of wealth, freedom, and adventure. They have settled in many parts of the Irish diaspora where their offspring have contributed greatly to their countries. While the family have an ancient ancestry and noble lineage, they also play a major part today in many areas of human endeavour across the globe.

Page numbers in *italic* refer to illustrations

PICTURE CREDITS

The publishers are grateful to the individual photographers and institutions who have made illustrations available for this book, as follows:

Chrysalis Books Archive: 6, 8, 9 (top), 9 (bottom), 11, 15 (top), 15 (bottom), 16, 20, 21, 24 (top), 24 (bottom), 33, 34 (bottom), 35, 36, 41 (top), 42, 44, 51

Corbis: 1, 2, 13 (top), 13 (bottom), 14, 18, 19 (top), 19 (bottom), 22, 25, 28, 30, 32, 37, 38 (top), 39, 40, 41 (bottom), 48, 49, 50 (top), 54, 55, 56, 57, 59, 60 (bottom), 61

Mary Evans Picture Library: 10, 26 (top), 38 (bottom), 46, 47, 50 (bottom), 52

Hulton|Archive: 12, 26 (bottom), 27, 34 (top), 43, 45, 53, 58 (top), 58 (bottom), 60 (top)

Antony Shaw: 23